The castle

This is the castle.
It is big.
It is old.
It is big and old.

The King

I am the King.
I live in the castle.
The castle is big.
It is big and old.

The Queen

I am the Queen.
I live in the castle.
The castle is old.
It is old and big.

The baby

This is the baby.
The baby lives in the castle.
The castle is big.
It is big. It is old.

The big guard

I am a guard.
I am a big guard.
I live in the castle.
It is big. It is old.

The little guard

I am a guard.
I am a little guard.
I live in the castle.
It is big and old.

We live in the castle.

It is a big castle.
It is big and old.

1. Am I the King?

2. Am I the Queen?

3. Am I the baby?

4. Is this the big guard?

5. Is this the little guard?

6. Is this the castle?

7. Is the castle old?

8. Is the castle big?